Medica

A Healthy Dose o

Compiled by Hugh Morrison

Montpelier Publishing

London

2015

ISBN-13: 978-1514717882

ISBN-10: 1514717883

Published by Montpelier Publishing, London.

Cover image by Viacheslav Lakobchuk

Printed by Amazon Createspace.

A man was describing his recent heart operation to a friend. 'I found myself going through a long narrow corridor, with a bright light at the end of it. Suddenly a man dressed in white appeared, and said to me, "go back, go back, it's not your time, you must go back"'. 'Good Lord!' said his friend. 'You've had one of those near death experiences!' 'Not exactly,' said the man. 'It was just the doctor coming out of the theatre to tell me the operation had been cancelled.'

'I was in hospital the other week. Terrible. Touch and go, it was – touch and go. The doctors said if touched one more nurse, I'd have to go.'

A man went to the dentist with terrible tooth decay. 'Last time you were here I told you to use floss on your teeth every night,' said the dentist with a sigh. 'You do know what floss is, don't you?' 'Sure,' replied the man. 'It's that pink stuff you get at the fairground.'

They used to say 'an apple a day keeps the doctor away.' Nowadays doctors' receptionists do it instead.

Rough patient: I don't want no injection, doc. I got a terrible fear of needles.

Doctor: Just relax and pretend you're at the tattooist's.

Doctor: I've been going through your records Mr Smith, and I'm afraid it's not good.

Mr Smith: What's the trouble?

Doctor: What on earth were you thinking of when you bought Barry Manilow's greatest hits?

A fat man wanted to lose weight so he went to the doctor who made him stand on the scales. The man sucked his tummy in. 'That won't help you,' said the doctor. 'Yes it will,' said the man, 'I can see the numbers now.'

Patient: Doctor, I haven't been able to eat, sleep or drink for a week. What have I got?

Doctor: Hunger, insomnia and thirst, I should think.

Concerned about his son who was an agrophobic and chronic hoarder, a man eventually persuaded a doctor to pay a home visit. Afterwards the man phoned the doctor to find out how he'd got on. 'I'm sorry but your son has so many mens' health issues that I was unable to help him,' replied the doctor. 'Surely you could have done something!' replied the man. 'Not really,' said the doctor. 'They were in a big pile in front of the door and I couldn't squeeze past them.'

A hysterical woman burst into the office of a hypnotherapist.

'Doctor, you must help me!' she cried. 'I've been faithful to my husband for twenty five years, but last night I slept with a complete stranger. I feel so guilty – you must hypnotise me so that I forget all about it!'

The doctor sighed and said 'not you again...'

Patient: Is Doctor Who a real person?

Nurse: Of course not. Why do you ask?

Patient: Well every time the receptionist says to someone 'Doctor Srinivasaraghavan will see you now,' people answer 'Doctor Who?'

'I've experienced quite a few heart-stopping moments in my job over the years,' said the doctor. 'I suppose that's why I'm being struck off.'

Doctor: I have some bad news and some very bad news.

Patient: Give me the bad news first.

Doctor: We have your test results. They say you have 24 hours to live.

Patient: That's terrible! What's the very bad news?

Doctor: I've been trying to reach you since yesterday.

My doctor said that jogging could add years to my life.

I didn't believe him at first, but I went yesterday and I feel ten years older already.

Newsflash: A surgeon has been fined £75,000 by the British Medical Council for removing the spleen of a patient instead of his gallbladder.

Speaking at the tribunal, the surgeon said, 'I am very sorry for the mistake, and I mean that from the bottom of that red, wobbly, pumping thing just above my tummy.'

A man phoned his doctor and said in a panicked voice, 'My wife is pregnant, and her contractions are only two minutes apart!'

'Is this her first child?' the doctor asked.

'No, you idiot!' shouted the man. 'This is her husband!'

'Doctor, can you cure my sleepwalking?' 'Try these.' 'Are they sleeping pills?' 'No. They're drawing pins. Put some on the floor by your bed.'

Prisoner: Look here, doctor! You've already removed my spleen, tonsils, adenoids, and one of my kidneys. I only came to see if you could get me out of this place!

Doctor: I am, bit by bit.

Patient: How much to have this tooth taken out?

Dentist: £100.00.

Patient: £100.00 for just a few minutes work?

Dentist: Well, I can extract it very slowly if you prefer.

Patient: Doctor, I think I swallowed a pillow.

Doctor: How do you feel?

Patient: A little down in the mouth.

Dentist (to patient): Could you help me? Could you give out a few of your loudest, most painful screams?

Patient: Why? I'm not in pain.

Dentist: It's just that there are lots of people in the waiting room, and I don't want to miss the five o'clock train.

Receptionist: Doctor, there is an invisible man in your waiting room.

Doctor: Tell him I can't see him.

A patient going into hospital saw two white coated doctors searching through the flower beds.

'Excuse me,' said the man, 'have you lost something?'

'No,' replied one of the doctors. 'We're doing a heart transplant for a tax inspector and want to find a suitable stone.'

Patient: My little boy believes in preventative medicine, doctor.

Doctor: Oh, really?

Patient: Yes, he tries to prevent me from making him take it!

A doctor and a policeman were called to attend a man who had collapsed in the street.

Doctor: We need to get this man to a hospital now!

Policeman: What is it?

Doctor: It's a big building with a lot of doctors in it.

Dizzy blonde: My stomach is getting awfully big, doctor.

Doctor: You ought to diet.

Dizzy blonde: Really? What colour?

A man was at the doctor's having a prostate examination.

'Don't be embarrassed', said the doctor. 'Taking the trousers off is normal for this type of procedure.'

'Erm...OK', replied the man. 'Should I take mine off as well?'

A specialist cured a wealthy man of chronic illness. 'I can never thank you enough, doctor,' said the man. 'But as a symbol of my gratitude, I've made a small change to my will to include you.' 'That's wonderful,' replied the doctor. 'By the way, can I have the prescription I just gave you - I just need to make a small change to that, too.'

Patient: I get so frightened during driving tests!

Doctor: Don't worry about it. You'll pass eventually.

Patient: But I'm the examiner!

Patient: Doctor, I have a serious memory problem. I can't remember anything!

Doctor: How long have you had this problem?

Patient: What problem?

Doctor (to Patient): Don't worry about your heart. It will function as long as you live.

Patient: Doctor, I think I need glasses.

Woman: You certainly do! This is a bank.

Sign on dentists' door: 'Smile. You might be doing this for the last time'.

Smith: I'm taking a rest cure.

Jones: What does that involve?

Smith: For three hours a day I have to sit in the doctor's waiting room until he can see me.

Smith: I saw that Harley Street specialist about my loss of memory.

Jones: What did he do?

Smith: He made me pay him in advance.

Sign outside cosmetic surgery clinic: 'If life gives you lemons, we'll give you melons.'

Doctor: Please bend your knee.

Patient: Which way?

Nurse: Doctor, we have lost our patient.

Doctor: What happened?

Nurse: He recovered.

Mrs McTavish: The doctor told me I need two weeks' complete rest: first in the south of France for the warm climate, then in the Swiss alps for the fresh air. Where are you going to take me first?

McTavish: To another doctor.

'Doctor, doctor, I keep thinking I'm a spider. Have you got anything to help me out?' 'Wait there, I'll get a glass and sheet of paper.'

A pretty young receptionist was setting up a new computer for a lecherous old doctor and she told him 'It's asking for a password. What would you like me to use?' The doctor replied, with a leer, 'How about 'my penis'? Calmly the receptionist typed it but then said 'What a pity. It says "password not long enough."'

McNab phoned the dentist to enquire about the cost for a tooth extraction.

'85 pounds for an extraction, sir' the dentist replied.

'85 quid! Huv ye no' got anythin' cheaper?'

'That's the normal charge,' said the dentist.

'Whit aboot if ye didnae use any anaesthetic?'

'That's unusual, sir, but I could do it and would knock 15 pounds off.'

'Whit aboot if ye used one of your trainees and still without any anaesthetic?'

'I can't guarantee the work, and it'll be painful. But the price could drop by 20 pounds.'

'How aboot if ye make it a trainin' session, and ye had yer student do the extraction with the other students watchin' and learnin'?'

'It'll be good for the students', reflected the dentist. 'I'll charge you 5 pounds but it will be traumatic.'

'Och, that's better – it's a deal,' said McNab. 'Can ye confirm an appointment for the wife next Tuesday then?'

Sign in STD clinic: 'Family planning advice - use rear entrance.'

Fat lady (to dietician). Is there any simple exercise to help me lose weight?

Dietician: Yes. You must move your head to the right and the left at a particular time.

Fat lady: At which particular time?

Dietician: Whenever anybody offers you food.

Doctor: I'm afraid you must prepare for the worst.

Patient: Isn't there anything that can be done, doctor?

Doctor: Well, you could try a course of mud baths.

Patient: Mud baths? Will that cure me?

Doctor: No, but it will get you used to the idea of being covered in earth.

An elderly doctor was on a house call to a woman who was in terrible pain. The doctor came out of the bedroom a minute after he'd gone in and asked the husband for a hammer. The puzzled husband went to the garage, and returned with a hammer. The doctor thanked him and went back into the bedroom. A moment later, he came out and asked, 'Do you have a chisel?' The man complied with the request. Ten minutes later the doctor asked for and received a pair of pliers, a screwdriver and a hacksaw. Finally the exasperated husband cried 'for God's sake man, what are you doing in there to my wife?' 'Nothing yet,' said the doctor. 'I'm just trying to get my instrument bag open.'

A Harley Street doctor and a prominent barrister were talking at a party. Their conversation was constantly interrupted by people describing their illnesses and asking the doctor for free medical advice.

After an hour of this, the exasperated doctor asked the barrister, 'How do you stop people from asking you for legal advice when you're out of the office?' 'I give it to them,' replied the barrister,' and then I send them a bill.'

The doctor was surprised, but agreed to give it a try. The next day, feeling slightly guilty, the doctor prepared the bills. When he went to post them, he found on his doormat a bill from the barrister.

A man twisted his ankle and was told by his doctor to soak it in hot water to relieve the swelling. When he got home he tried it, but the swelling got worse. His wife said 'It sounds a bit odd to me. I always thought you were supposed to use cold water.' The man tried cold water instead and the swelling went down.

Confused, the man phoned his doctor. 'Look here,' said the man. 'What sort of doctor are you? You told me to soak my ankle in hot water and it got worse. My wife told me to try cold water, and it got better.' 'I don't understand it,' replied the doctor. 'I'm sure my wife said to use hot water.'

Patient: I'm having trouble with my breathing.

Doctor: We'll soon put a stop to that.

Doctor: How can you prevent disease from biting insects?

Student: Don't bite any.

A doctor was walking through his surgery when he saw a nun rush out of one of the examining rooms in a hysterical state. He went into the room and asked what happened. 'Ah,' replied his colleague. 'That was Sister Immaculata from the nunnery. I just told her she was pregnant'. 'My God,' replied the first doctor. 'Is she?' 'Of course not,' replied the other doctor. 'But I've certainly cured her hiccups.'

Smith (in hospital ward): What are you in for?

Jones: Ingrowing toenails.

Smith: Ouch! When I had that done, I couldn't walk for a week.

Jones: Oh dear. What are you in for?

Smith: Circumcision.

Jones: Ouch! I had that done when I was born, and I couldn't walk for a year!

An unemployed chef claimed he couldn't work because he'd lost his sense of taste. In order to continue receiving benefits, he had to attend a medical exam. The doctor said 'I'm going to pour liquid number 22 on your tongue. Please tell me if you can taste anything.' He poured some fluid on the man's tongue, who spat it out with a disgusted expression, and shouted 'That's urine!' 'Congratulations, your sense of taste is back!' said the doctor.

A few weeks later the chef returned. This time he claimed he couldn't work due to memory loss. The doctor said to the nurse, 'Liquid number 22 please.' 'That's for loss of taste,' said the man in horror. 'Congratulations,' said the doctor. 'Your memory is back too.'

A class of first year pathology students were looking at a corpse for the first time. 'In pathology it is necessary to have two important qualities as a doctor,' said the professor. The first is that you should not be disgusted by anything to do with corpses. As an example, the professor stuck his finger in the corpse's rectum, withdrew it and then stuck his finger in his mouth. The students recoiled in horror. 'Now,' he said to the class, 'do the same thing.' After some hesitation the students lined up and one by one repeated the procedure. When everyone had finished and was looking distinctly ill, the professor looked at them and said, 'The second most important quality is observation. I stuck my middle finger in the body and put my index finger in my mouth. Now learn to pay attention.'

Doctor: I'm afraid, Mr Jones, that there's no magic bullet that can solve the problems you're having with your wife.

Mr Jones: Who needs a magic one?

'There's nothing really wrong with you,' said the doctor to his patient. 'Just drink a glass of this tonic each night followed by a hot bath and you'll be right as rain.' The next day the doctor returned to check on the man who looked worse than ever. 'Did you drink the tonic?' asked the doctor. 'Yes,' said the man, 'but I could only manage to drink half the hot bath.'

Smith: How did you get on at the doctor?

Jones: Bad news I'm afraid. I've got to take a tablet every day for the rest of my life.

Smith: That doesn't sound too bad, what are you worried about?

Jones: He only gave me three tablets!

'Doctor, I'm thinking of getting a vasectomy.'

'That's a big decision. Have you discussed it with your family?'

'Yes, we took a vote, and they're in favour of it 15 to 2.'

Patient: I've got a terrible phobia about trains.

Doctor: Are you taking anything for it?

Patient: Yes, the bus.

'This time last year, the doctor gave me just one month to live. That's the last time I trust a Mayan doctor.'

A school-leaver went to a careers advisor and said he wanted to become a doctor. 'A noble profession,' said the advisor, 'and one that would suit someone with your qualifications. 'However I would advise you to change your name first, Mr Acula.'

I went to the doctor's about my superiority complex. He said there was nothing I could do to help him.

Patient: I keep dreaming that beautiful women are throwing themselves at me, but that I keep pushing them away.

Doctor: Well, what do you want me to do about it?

Patient: Break my arm.

Then there was the man who swallowed a white snooker ball, and was told by the doctor to go to the front of the cue.

An alcoholic, a compulsive eater and a hypochondriac were sitting in a doctor's waiting room.

'I'm so tired and thirsty, I must have a glass of whisky,' said the alcoholic.

'I'm so tired and thirsty, I must have a double milk shake,' said the compulsive eater.

'I'm so tired and thirsty,' said the hypochondriac, 'I must have diabetes.'

What's the easiest way to add insult to injury? Write something rude on a plaster cast.

Stan feared his wife Mavis wasn't hearing as well as she used to and he thought she might need a hearing aid. Not quite sure how to approach her, he called the doctor to discuss the problem.

The doctor told him there was a simple informal test the husband could perform before bothering with a full examination in the surgery.

'Here's what you do,' said the Doctor. 'Stand about 20 feet away from her, and in a normal conversational speaking tone see if she hears you. If not, go to 10 feet, then 5 feet, and so on until you get a response.'

That evening, Mavis was in the kitchen cooking dinner and Stan was in the living room, about 20 feet away. He decided to try the test. 'What's for dinner, Mavis?' he said.

No response.

So he moved closer to the kitchen, and repeated 'Mavis, what's for dinner?' Still no response.

Next he moved right into the kitchen, just five feet behind his wife, and said 'Mavis, what's for dinner?'

Again he gets no response.

Finally he walked right up behind her. 'Mavis, what's for dinner?'

'FOR THE FOURTH TIME STAN, IT'S SHEPHERD'S PIE!'

Doctor: I haven't seen you for a long time.

Patient: I know, I've been ill.

Farmer Giles was complaining to a friend about his new bull. 'All that bull does is eat grass. Won't even look at a cow.'

'Take him to the vet,' his friend suggested.

The next week, Farmer Giles was much happier. 'The vet gave him some pills, and the bull serviced all of my cows!' he told his friend.

'Then he broke through the fence and bred with all my neighbour's cows!'

'What kind of pills were they?' asked the friend.

'I don't know,' said the farmer,' but they've got a minty taste.'

Doctor: Do you want the good news or the bad news first?

Patient: Give me the good news.

Doctor: You're going to have a disease named after you.

Paddy was at a Dublin specialist for an examination. The nurse handed him a small plastic bottle and told him to urinate in it.

'Sure and not in front of all these people?' said Paddy in a shocked voice.

'Certainly not,' replied the nurse, pointing to the lavatory. 'Do it in that room.'

A few minutes later Paddy emerged and handed the nurse the empty bottle.

'Turns out I didn't need it,' he said. 'There was a toilet in there.'

A politician was on a tour of a psychiatric hospital. He asked the director how they decided if a patient needed to be committed.

'Well,' the director said, 'we fill a bath with water, then offer the patient a teaspoon, a teacup and a bucket, and ask him to empty the tub.'

'I see,' the politician said. 'A normal person would use the bucket because it's the biggest.'

'No,' the director said. 'A normal person would pull the plug.'

Doctor: I'm referring you to a proctologist, but he's very busy - it may be a while before you can see him.

Patient: Well tell him to pull his finger out!

Doctor (to receptionist): Have you seen my auroscope?

Receptionist: No! Does it say anything good?

Bert and Mavis were getting married at the grand old ages of 95 and 94 respectively.

Before the wedding, they visited the local chemist.

'Do you sell heart medication?' asked Bert.

'Of course,' replied the chemist.

'What about pills for arthritis and lumbago?' asked Mavis.

'Certainly,' the chemist said.

'How about corn plasters, surgical stockings and back rests?' enquired Bert.

'Yes, we've got all those,' the chemist said.

'Do you have wheelchairs and zimmer frames?' asked Mavis.

'We've got plenty of those in the back room,' replied the chemist.

'That's great,' said Bert. 'There's just one more question.'

'What's that?' asked the chemist, wondering what on earth more they could require.

'Can we have our wedding list here?'

Patient: I'm very worried about my brother, doctor. He thinks he's an orange.

Psychiatrist: Well you'd better fetch him here and I'll examine him.

Patient: There's no need, doctor. I've got him here in my pocket!

Coroner: What were your husband's last words?

Widow: 'I don't see how they can make a profit on vodka that costs 99p a bottle.'

A man went to an eminent psychiatrist complaining that unknown assailants were lurking under his bed every night. 'I can certainly cure you of these delusions,' said the doctor. 'Come and see me next week.' The next week the man reappeared and announced himself cured. 'How is that possible, we haven't even had a session of analysis,' said the doctor. 'Simple,' said the man. 'I sawed the legs off my bed.'

A country GP received a call from an anxious patient on a remote farm who was suffering from fever with a high temperature. He demanded the doctor visit him immediately.

'You must give me a thermometer reading first' said the doctor.

'Why?'

'Because if it's too cold over there I'm not going out'.

Things were a bit confused at the medical practice because a new wing was being built. A man came into the doctor's surgery and said 'I'm here about the piles, doctor, what should I do?' 'Drop your trousers and bend over the couch, please,' said the doctor, without looking up from his paperwork. The man began to protest but the doctor reassured him, 'I do this all the time. It's absolutely nothing to worry about.' 'Well, if you say so, doctor,' said the man, and undressed. During the digital rectal examination, the man said 'I'm not really sure why this is necessary, doctor, but don't be too long because the pile driver's parked on a double yellow line.'

Doctor: Are you urinating more easily this morning, Mr Jones?

Mr Jones: Yes – I've been practicing all night!

I had an MRI last night
It left me quite bereft;
In my left brain nothing's right
And in my right brain nothing's left.

A brief history of medicine:

2000 BC: Here, eat this root.

1000 AD: That root is heathen. Say this prayer.

1840 AD: That prayer is superstition. Drink this potion.

1940 AD: That potion is a placebo. Swallow this pill.

1985 AD: That pill is ineffective. Take this antibiotic.

2015 AD: That antibiotic is artificial. Here, eat this root.

Journalist (to Harley Street surgeon): To what do you attribute your rapid rise in your career?

Surgeon: It has always been my rule never to perform an operation unless I was sure it would be a success either way.

Patient: 'I'm in so much pain I want to die.'

Doctor: 'You did the right thing to call me.'

A doctor engaged a builder to construct a new path for his house. The doctor went away for three days and when he returned found the builder waiting for his money.

The doctor was not satisfied with his work and said 'Look here — the path is covered with gravel and earth, and in my estimation it's a bad job.'

The builder looked at him in surprise for a moment and replied: 'I'll bet there's many a bad job of yours covered with gravel and earth as well!'

Barrister (to doctor): What side should I lie on?

Doctor: The side that's paying you the most.

My wife had a facelift the other day. They didn't lift it high enough –
I can still see it.

'You must give up coffee and — '

'I never drink it, doctor.'

'And stop smoking.'

'I don't smoke.'

'Humph! that's bad. If you haven't anything to give up, I'm afraid I
can't do much for you.'

The curator of the museum was classifying Egyptian curios. He
observed a perplexed expression on the face of his young assistant.

'What seems to be the matter?' he asked. 'Is there anything you
don't understand?'

'Yes, sir,' answered the helper. 'Here is a papyrus on which the
characters are so badly traced that they are indecipherable. How
shall I classify it?'

'Let me see,' said the curator, examining the piece. 'Just call it a
doctor's prescription in the time of Pharaoh.'

Dr Smith: 'How's your new receptionist?'

Dr Jones: 'Highly efficient. I haven't seen a patient all week!'

A private surgeon was about to perform a serious operation on a nervous patient.

'Now don't worry old chap,' said the surgeon. 'I've performed hundreds of operations like this one.'

'You must be a very rich man then,' said the patient. 'Not really,' replied the surgeon. 'I only get paid by the patients who survive.'

Doctor: Don't you know that smoking shortens your life?

Patient: I'm not so sure. My father smokes 60 a day, and he's eighty years old this year.

Doctor: Well if he'd never smoked he might have been ninety by now!

A miser was convinced he needed medical help from top private doctors, but was too mean to pay for it. One day he was seated next to a Harley Street doctor at a dinner party. He contrived to introduce the matter of his illness into the conversation, dropping lots of hints. After none of these worked he came straight out and asked the wearied doctor what he should take for it.

'Professional advice,' came the reply.

Not to be put off so easily, the miser persisted.

'But what would you take for it?' the miser asked.

'A fee,' said the doctor.

An obese man was advised by his doctor that he should regularly go for a walk on an empty stomach.

'Yes, but whose stomach should I walk on?' replied the confused patient.

Paddy was seeing a psychiatrist. The doctor showed him a book of Rorschach inkblots.

'What does this remind you of?' said the doctor.

'Sex,' said Paddy without hesitation.

The doctor flipped the page. 'And this one?'

'Sex,' replied Paddy again.

Turning to another page, the doctor asked again. ⏺

'What about this one.''Sex.'

This went on for some time until the doctor had gone through several books of inkblots.

'You appear to have an obsession with sex,' said the doctor, finally.

'Huh!' said Paddy in disgust. 'You're the one with all the dirty books.'

A prison doctor was discussing a prisoner's test results.

'I've got some good news and some bad news, prisoner 15447,' said the doctor.

'What's the good news?'

'You'll be out of here in a week.'

Prisoner 15447 was amazed. 'But doc, I'm supposed to be here for the rest of my life!'

'Ah,' said the doctor awkwardly. 'That brings me on to the bad news...'

'Do you think I shall live until I'm ninety, doctor?'

'How old are you now?'

'Forty.'

'Do you drink, smoke, take drugs, or go with loose women?'

'Certainly not. I've no vices of any kind.'

'Well, what do you want to live another fifty years for?'

Sir Samuel Garth, physician to George I, was a member of the infamous Kit-Kat Club. Coming to the club one night, he said he must soon be gone, having many patients to attend; but some good wine was produced, and he forgot them. The author Sir Richard Steele was one of the party, and reminded him of the visits he had to pay. Garth pulled out his list, which amounted to fifteen, and said, 'It's no great matter whether I see them tonight or not; for nine of them, have such bad constitutions that all the physicians in the world can't save them; and the other six have such good constitutions that all the physicians in the world can't kill them.'

Doctor: Have you ever had chicken pox?

Rough patient: No, I've had chicken nuggets though.

In Victorian London a physician treated a man who had a reputation as being very careful with his money.

After the man had miraculously recovered, his wife visited the doctor and presented him with a beautiful embroidered purse.

'Please accept this as a token of my appreciation. It is handmade.'

The doctor sighed as he looked at the purse.

'It's very pretty, ma'am, but presents only maintain friendship. They don't maintain families.'

'What is your fee?' asked the wife.

'Five guineas,' replied the doctor.

The woman opened the purse and removed ten guineas. She put back five, and gave it to the doctor.

Doctor: I can't find any reason for your headaches. Perhaps it's because of excessive drinking?

Patient: Alright, I'll come back later when you've sobered up a bit.

Man: Doctor, I'm suffering terribly from chronic ear-ache, stress, and lack of sexual desire. I've seen dozens of doctors but nobody can help.

Doctor: I'm referring you to a specialist.

Man: Not *another* doctor?

Doctor: No, a divorce lawyer.

A member of the faculty in a London medical college was appointed an honorary physician to the Queen. He proudly wrote a notice on the blackboard in his classroom:

'Professor Jennings informs his students that he has been appointed honorary physician to Her Majesty Queen Elizabeth the Second.' ⏎

When he returned to the class-room in the afternoon he found written below his notice this line:

'God save the Queen.'

The henpecked husband of a hypochondriac wife was despatched to the chemist's shop with a prescription.

Knowing the lady well, the pharmacist gave the medicine to the man and said 'Run back home as fast as you can. Don't stop for anything.'

'Good heavens,' replied the husband. 'Is it as bad as all that?'

'Certainly,' said the chemist. 'If you don't, she's likely to be better by the time you get back and you'll have wasted your money.'

A case was being heard where a private doctor had been accused of overcharging a patient. A nurse was asked whether she thought the doctor did not make several visits after the patient was out of danger. 'No,' replied the nurse. 'I considered the patient in danger as long as the doctor continued his visits.'

A man was hit by a car and lay in the road moaning in pain. The driver jumped out and said 'You're lucky. We're in front of a doctor's surgery.' 'Yes,' groaned the man. 'Except I'm the doctor.'

Surgeon (to patient): Why are you so nervous?

Patient: Well doctor, it's my first operation.

Surgeon: Really? It's mine as well, but I feel fine.

An old lady returned to her doctor and reported that constipation was still troubling her. 'What about the suppositories I prescribed?' asked the doctor. 'They didn't do any good,' said the lady, 'even though I swallowed the lot.'

Dermatologist: Do you take baths or showers?

Patient: Yes.

Patient: Doctor, I need your help. I think I'm a moth.

Doctor: You don't need me, you need a psychiatrist.

Patient: I know, but your light was on.

An elderly woman went to the doctor complaining of a pain in her right knee. 'There's nothing I can do,' said the doctor. 'It's just old age.' 'In that case,' said the woman, 'why doesn't my other knee hurt as well?'

A medical student was told to remove the spleen from a cadaver. After he did, he kept fumbling around.

'What are you doing?' asked the professor.

The student answered, 'Looking for the other one.'

'Doctor, doctor, I've swallowed a bone!' 'Are you choking?' 'No, I really did!'

A woman took her elderly husband, who was having heart problems, to the surgery. The doctor gave him some pills and said 'take one pill on Mondays, Tuesdays and Wednesdays. You can skip the rest of the week.' Two weeks later the doctor was called to the man's house to give a death certificate. 'I can't understand it,' said the doctor to the grieving widow. 'Didn't he take the pills?' 'Oh yes,' said the woman. 'But I think it was the skipping that killed him.'

Doctor: Don't forget to stick your tongue out when the nurse comes.

Patient: Why?'

Doctor: I don't like her'

A beautiful young woman was about to have an operation. She was put on a trolley and left in the corridor to wait until the surgeons arrived. A young man in a white coat came over, lifted up the sheet and examined her naked body. He walked away and talked to another man in a white coat, who came over and performed the same examination. Then a third man came over and lifted the sheet. The woman said 'Are these examinations strictly necessary?'I've no idea,' said one of the men. 'We're just here to paint the ceiling.'

A man went to the doctor's and asked for a double dose of Viagra. 'Why do you need so much?' asked the concerned doctor. 'Well,' said the man, 'my girlfriend is coming over on Friday, my other girlfriend wants me to visit her on Saturday, and to celebrate my birthday I've booked a call girl for Sunday.' The doctor raised an eyebrow but gave the prescription anyway. On Monday morning the man re-appeared at the surgery with his right arm in a sling and said 'Nobody showed up!'

Doctor: I have some bad news Mr Jones. Your wife's come down with something.

Mr Jones: What is it?

Doctor: The plane and the rest of the passengers.

Newsflash: A Cambridge University research group which advertised for participants in a study of obsessive-compulsive disorder has had an overwhelming response. They have received 4,786 replies to their online appeal. All from the same person.

Three patients in a mental institution were preparing for an examination given by the chief psychiatrist. He explained that if they passed the exam, they would be pronounced sane and allowed to leave.

The doctor took the patients to the top of a diving board overlooking an empty swimming pool, and asked the first patient to jump.

The first patient jumped head first into the pool and broke both arms.

The second patient jumped and broke both legs.

The third patient looked over the side of the pool and refused to jump.

'Congratulations!' said the doctor. 'You can now go free. But tell me, why didn't you jump?'

'Simple,' said the man. 'I can't swim.'

Patient: Doctor, I have terrible diarrhoea. What can I do to stop it?

Doctor: Have you tried lemons?

Patient: Yes, but they kept falling out.

Newsflash: NHS hospital closures have led to a new type of bypass operation being carried out. Finance chiefs are happy but doctors have raised concerns about being hit by cars on the bypass.

Patient: You've got to help me - I just can't stop my hands shaking.

Doctor: Do you drink a lot?

Patient: Not really - I spill most of it!

Patent: I keep seeing spots before my eyes

Opthalmologist: Didn't the new glasses help?

Patient: Not really - now the spots are clearer!

A mechanic was working under the bonnet of a car when he spotted a world-famous heart surgeon in his garage collecting his Ferrari. The mechanic approached the doctor and said, 'Doctor, look at this engine. I take valves out, fix them, put in new parts and when I finish this it will work just like a new one. So how come I earn a fraction of what you get for doing basically the same work?'

The surgeon paused, then replied 'Try doing it with the engine running!'

Dentist: For God's sake, stop making those noises and waving your arms. I haven't even touched your tooth yet.

Patient: Yes, I know. But you're standing on my foot.

A man who had just undergone a very complicated operation kept complaining about a bump on his head and a terrible headache. Since he had had a stomach operation, there was no explanation for it. Finally his doctor spoke to surgeon about it.

The surgeon replied, 'Nothing to worry about. He probably does have a bump on his head. About halfway through the operation we ran out of anaesthetic.'

Newsflash: 20,000 viagra tablets were stolen last night from a pharmacy in south London. Police are looking for a gang of hardened criminals.

Doctor: Don't you know alcohol is a slow poison?

Patient: That's alright, I'm not in a hurry!

Fat patient: I can't help being overweight. The problem is, obesity runs in my family.

Doctor: No, the problem is *nobody* runs in your family.

Did you hear about the prostitute that had her appendix out? The doctor sewed up the wrong hole. Fortunately she's still able to make some money on the side.

Newsflash: A Californian company is developing some computer chips that enable music to be played through women's breast implants. This is a major breakthrough for women who complain that men stare at their breasts and don't listen to them.

Medical howlers from doctors' case notes

The patient has no previous history of suicides.

Patient has left her white blood cells at another hospital.

The injury was sustained when the patient was put on a trolley by a nurse who then pulled him off.

The patient was found in possession of drag paraphernalia.

I saw your patient today, who is still under our car for physical therapy.

The lab test indicated abnormal lover function.

On the second day the knee was better and on the third day it disappeared.

The patient is tearful and crying constantly. She also appears to be depressed.

The patient has been depressed since she began seeing me in 1998.

She is numb from her toes down.

I performed resuscitation after the patient was found floating in the poo.

While in casualty, she was examined, x-rated and sent home.

Occasional, constant infrequent headaches.

Patient was alert and unresponsive.

Rectal examination revealed a normal size thyroid.

Examination of genitalia reveals that he is circus sized.

Skin: somewhat pale, but present.

The pelvic exam will be done later on the floor.

When she fainted, her eyes rolled around the room.

Between you and me, we ought to be able to get this lady pregnant.

By the time he was admitted, his rapid heart had stopped, and he was feeling better.

The patient has an obstruction in his Euston Station tube.

Old Mr Jones hobbled into the doctor's surgery, bent double and walking slowly. After just a few minutes he emerged, walking completely upright.

Old Mr Smith was in the waiting room and said 'That must be a miracle doctor in there.' he exclaimed. 'What treatment did he give you? What's his secret?'

Mr Jones said 'Well, the doctor looked me up and down, analysed the situation, and gave me a walking stick that was four inches longer than the one I had been using.'

'They say "laughter is the best medicine". They've obviously never tried morphine.'

A famous surgeon went on a grouse shooting weekend in Scotland. When he came back, his colleagues asked him how it had been. 'Oh, it was very disappointing,' he said. 'I didn't kill a thing. I'd have been better off staying here in the hospital.'

Nurse: Doctor, the man you've just treated collapsed on the front step. What should I do?'

Doctor: Turn him around so it looks like he was just arriving.

Mrs Jones spoke to her doctor, very concerned about her husband's bad temper.

The doctor said 'I have a cure for that. When it seems that he is getting angry, just take a glass of water and start swishing it in your mouth. Just rinse, but don't swallow it until he either leaves the room or calms down.'

Two weeks later the woman returned to the doctor, looking very pleased.

'Doctor,' she said, 'that was marvellous! Every time my husband started losing his temper, I rinsed my mouth with water and he calmed down. How on earth does that work with just plain water?'

The doctor replied 'The water itself does nothing. It's keeping your mouth shut that does the trick.'

Doctor: Are you on HRT?

Rough patient: No, income support.

A hospital had a policy of putting on the patient's wristband any items that he or she was allergic to. A man visited his elderly mother on the ward. He noticed her wristband and said to a nurse angrily 'how dare you call my mother bananas!'

Doctor: I'm sorry to have to tell you that you may have rabies, and it could prove fatal.

Patient: Well, doctor, please give me a pen and paper.

Doctor: To make your will?

Patient: No, to make a list of people I want to bite.

Patient: Nurse, I keep seeing spots in front of my eyes.

Nurse: Have you seen a doctor?

Patient: No, just spots.

Patient: Doctor, my family thinks I'm mad!

Doctor: Why?

Patient: I like sausages.

Doctor: What's wrong with that? I like sausages too.

Patient: That's wonderful – you must come and see my collection, I've got thousands!

In the middle of the night there was a loud knocking on the doctor's door. He angrily thrust his head out of the window and said 'Well?' 'No,' replied the caller. 'Sick!'

Patient: Doctor, I have a terrible problem. I have a big house in Mayfair and a summer cottage in Tuscany. I've also got a yacht moored at Cannes. I drive a Bentley and my wife drives a Jaguar. Both my sons are at Eton and my daughter is at Roedean.

Psychiatrist: It sounds like a wonderful life – what's the problem?

Patient: I only earn £200 a week!

Doctor(to patient): I have some good news and bad news.

Patient: Give me the bad news first.

Doctor: You have only two weeks to live.

Patient: My God – what's the good news?

Doctor: Oh – that's for another patient.

'Doctor, I can't stop stealing things.'

'Take these tablets; if that doesn't work get me a flat screen TV.'

Three medical students were discussing what branch of medicine they were going to specialise in.

The first said 'I want to be a brain surgeon. It's exciting and where all the great discoveries are being made.'

The second said 'I'm going to be a heart surgeon. Think of all the lives I could save.'

The third said 'I'm going to be a dermatologist.'

'What on earth for?' asked the other two.

'Your patients never die, they never get well, and they never get you up in the middle of the night.'

Patient: Doctor, last night I was feeling so depressed, I tried to kill myself by taking 200 of those tablets from that bottle you prescribed.

Doctor: Good lord! How are you still alive?

Patient: Well after taking the first two, I felt much better.

Patient: Doctor, I've noticed one of my eyes looks different to the other.

Doctor: Which one?

A gynaecologist had become fed up with NHS cuts, stress and long working hours. He decided to become a mechanic instead and signed up for a training course. At the end of term he completed the exam. When the results came back, he was surprised to find that he had obtained a score of 150%. Fearing an error, he called the instructor and said 'I don't want to appear ungrateful for the result, but I wonder if there is an error in the grade?'

The instructor said, 'During the exam, you took the engine apart perfectly, which was worth 50% of the total mark. You put the engine back together again perfectly, which is also worth 50% of the mark.'

After a pause, the instructor added, 'I gave you an extra 50% because you managed to do it all through the exhaust pipe.'

Other titles from Montpelier Publishing

Available from Amazon

Humour and puzzles

The Book of Church Jokes

After Dinner Laughs

After Dinner Laughs 2

Scottish Jokes

Welsh Jokes

The Bumper Book of Riddles, Puzzles and Rhymes

Wedding Jokes

A Little Book of Limericks

Take My Wife: Hilarious Jokes of Love and Marriage

The Old Fashioned Joke Book

Men's interest

The Pipe Smoker's Companion

Advice to Gentlemen

The Frugal Gentleman

The Men's Guide to Frugal Grooming

The Real Ale Companion

The Cigar Collection

19375678R00025

Printed in Great Britain
by Amazon